# Musical Notes
# ROCK
# MUSIC HISTORY

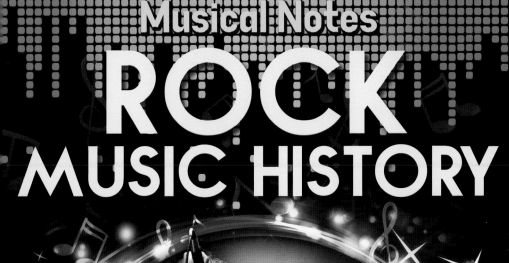

Kenny Abdo

Fly!
An Imprint of Abdo Zoom
abdobooks.com

# abdobooks.com

Published by Abdo Zoom, a division of ABDO, P.O. Box 398166, Minneapolis, Minnesota 55439. Copyright © 2020 by Abdo Consulting Group, Inc. International copyrights reserved in all countries. No part of this book may be reproduced in any form without written permission from the publisher. Fly!™ is a trademark and logo of Abdo Zoom.

Printed in the United States of America, North Mankato, Minnesota.
102019
012020

Photo Credits: Alamy, AP Images, Getty Images, iStock, Shutterstock
Production Contributors: Kenny Abdo, Jennie Forsberg, Grace Hansen
Design Contributors: Dorothy Toth, Neil Klinepier

**Library of Congress Control Number: 2019941320**

**Publisher's Cataloging-in-Publication Data**

Names: Abdo, Kenny, author.
Title: Rock music history / by Kenny Abdo
Description: Minneapolis, Minnesota : Abdo Zoom, 2020 | Series: Musical notes |
    Includes online resources and index.
Identifiers: ISBN 9781532129452 (lib. bdg.) | ISBN 9781098220433 (ebook) |
    ISBN 9781098220921 (Read-to-Me ebook)
Subjects: LCSH: Rock music--Juvenile literature. | Music and history--Juvenile
    literature. | Alternative pop/rock music--Juvenile literature. | Rock and roll music-
    Juvenile literature.
Classification: DDC 781.66--dc23

# TABLE OF CONTENTS

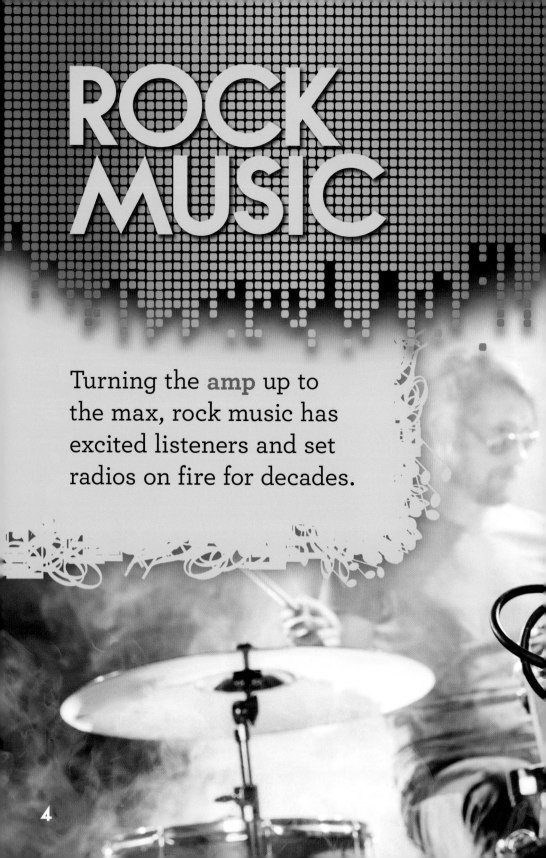

# ROCK MUSIC

Turning the **amp** up to the max, rock music has excited listeners and set radios on fire for decades.

Rock came onto the scene by mixing many American music **genres**. Combining rhythm and blues (R&B), country, and jazz, rock was like nothing else heard before.

# OPENING ACT

Alan Freed was a **disc jockey** in the 1950s. He was the first person to call certain records "rock and roll." Freed organized the first rock and roll concert in 1952 in Cleveland.

Bill Haley's "Rock Around the Clock" reached number one in 1955. This brought the **genre** into the spotlight. Musicians like Elvis Presley, Chuck Berry, and Jerry Lee Lewis began to release hit after hit.

# HEADLINER

In the 60s, bands from across the pond in the United Kingdom made a splash in America. The Beatles, The Rolling Stones, and The Kinks lit up the airwaves. Their sound was called the British Invasion.

During the 70s, groups like Pink Floyd, Queen, and Led Zeppelin became cultural **icons**. Each group had a distinct sound to their music.

14

15

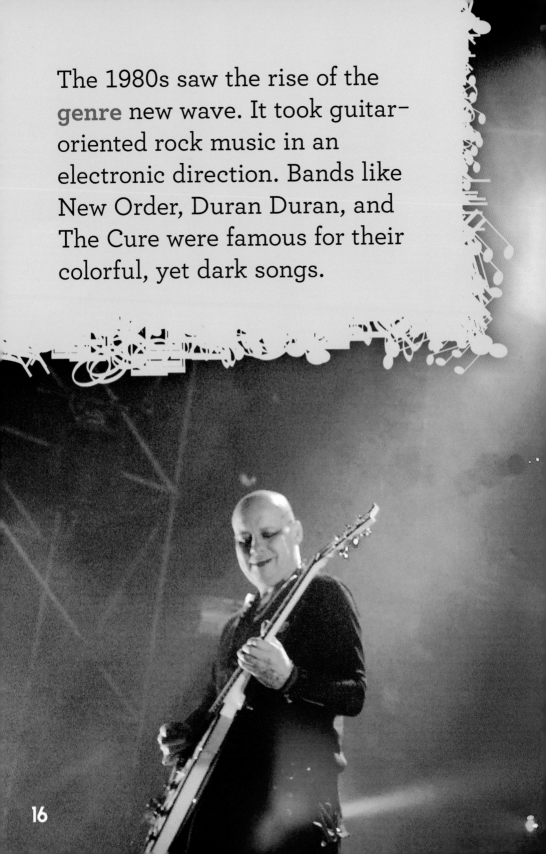

The 1980s saw the rise of the **genre** new wave. It took guitar-oriented rock music in an electronic direction. Bands like New Order, Duran Duran, and The Cure were famous for their colorful, yet dark songs.

Kurt Cobain's band, Nirvana, along with his wife Courtney Love's band, Hole, brought grunge music into the mainstream during the early 1990s. It was a style of music steeped in guitar distortion and feedback.

Greta Van Fleet is keeping rock alive. Their **debut** 2018 album, *Anthem of a Peaceful Army,* was a smash! It topped the Billboard Rock Album chart the week it was released. Their **EP** "From the Fires" won the Best Rock Album Grammy in 2019.

# GLOSSARY

**amplifier (amp)** – a plug-in loudspeaker used to amplify the sound of electrical instruments.

**debut** – a first appearance.

**disc jockey (DJ)** – a radio personality who introduces and plays popular music.

**distortion** – altering sound of an electric instrument to sound gritty and fuzzy.

**extended play record (EP)** – a record that is shorter in length than a typical music album.

**feedback** – when a microphone picks up a sound from a speaker and amplifies it, creating a high-pitched loop.

**genre** – a type of art, music, or literature.

**icon** – a celebrity whose fame and popularity stays the same or increases through time.

# ONLINE RESOURCES

**Booklinks**
**NONFICTION NETWORK**
**FREE!** ONLINE NONFICTION RESOURCES

To learn more about rock music history, please visit abdobooklinks.com or scan this QR code. These links are routinely monitored and updated to provide the most current information available.

# INDEX